WHERE PEOPLE LIVE

# LIFE IN A CITY

WRITTEN BY
Noah Leatherland

KidHaven PUBLISHING

Published in 2025 by
KidHaven Publishing, an Imprint of
Greenhaven Publishing, LLC
2544 Clinton St., Buffalo, NY 14224



**Written by:** Noah Leatherland
**Edited by:** Rebecca Phillips-Bartlett
**Designed by:** Jasmine Pointer



**Cataloging-in-Publication Data**

Names: Leatherland, Noah, 1999-.
Title: Life in a city / Noah Leatherland.
Description: Buffalo, NY : KidHaven Publishing, 2025. | Series: Where people live | Includes glossary and index.
Identifiers: ISBN 9781534549166 (pbk.) | ISBN 9781534549173 (library bound) | ISBN 9781534549180 (ebook)
Subjects: LCSH: Cities and towns--Juvenile literature. | Sociology, Urban--Juvenile literature.
Classification: LCC HT152.L38 2025 | DDC 307.76--dc23



Manufactured in the United States of America

CPSIA compliance information: Batch #CW25KH
For further information contact Greenhaven Publishing LLC
at 1-844-317-7404.

Please visit our website,
www.greenhavenpublishing.com.
For a free color catalog of all our high-quality books, call toll free 1-844-317-7404
or fax 1-844-317-7405.

Find us on

## IMAGE CREDITS

*All images are courtesy of Shutterstock.com. With thanks to Getty Images, Thinkstock Photo and iStockphoto.*
Cover – HappyPictures, Picksell, PIYATHILAKA, Nikolas_jkd. Alien Character – HappyPictures. Background throughout – Picksell. 4–5 – KeyFame, Ryan DeBerardinis, Sean Pavone, Kashif Hameed. 6–7 – Stephan Guarch, trabantos. 8–9 – Thomas La Mela, Andrey Bayda. 10–11 – DW labs Incorporated, Raul Rodriguez Arias, ColorMaker, Brian Goodman, TTstudio. 12–13 – BGStock72, Kleber Cordeiro, Microstocker.Pro. 14–15 – Tomas Kohoutek, NDAB Creativity. 16–17 – trekandshoot, stock_photo_world. 18–19 – Jaione_Garcia, Drazen Zigic, Microstocker.Pro. 20–21 – fizkes, Odua Images, Quarta. 22–23 – f11photo, New Vectors, 19 STUDIO, HappyPictures.

# CONTENTS



WORDS THAT LOOK LIKE THIS CAN BE FOUND IN THE GLOSSARY ON PAGE 24.

# WELCOME TO EARTH

Hello to everyone back home on the planet Morpia. My name is Morp. Welcome to another episode of *Where People Live* – the show where we explore Earth and the humans who live there.

Humans can be found living on almost every part of Earth. They have made **SETTLEMENTS** in hot, cold, dry, and wet places. Sometimes, these settlements grow so big that they become cities.

WHAT **HUMANS** MEAN

**SETTLEMENTS:** Anywhere that a group of people builds a place to live

# WHAT ON EARTH IS A CITY?

There are lots of humans living in the city – many more than in a village or most towns. So, what is a city?

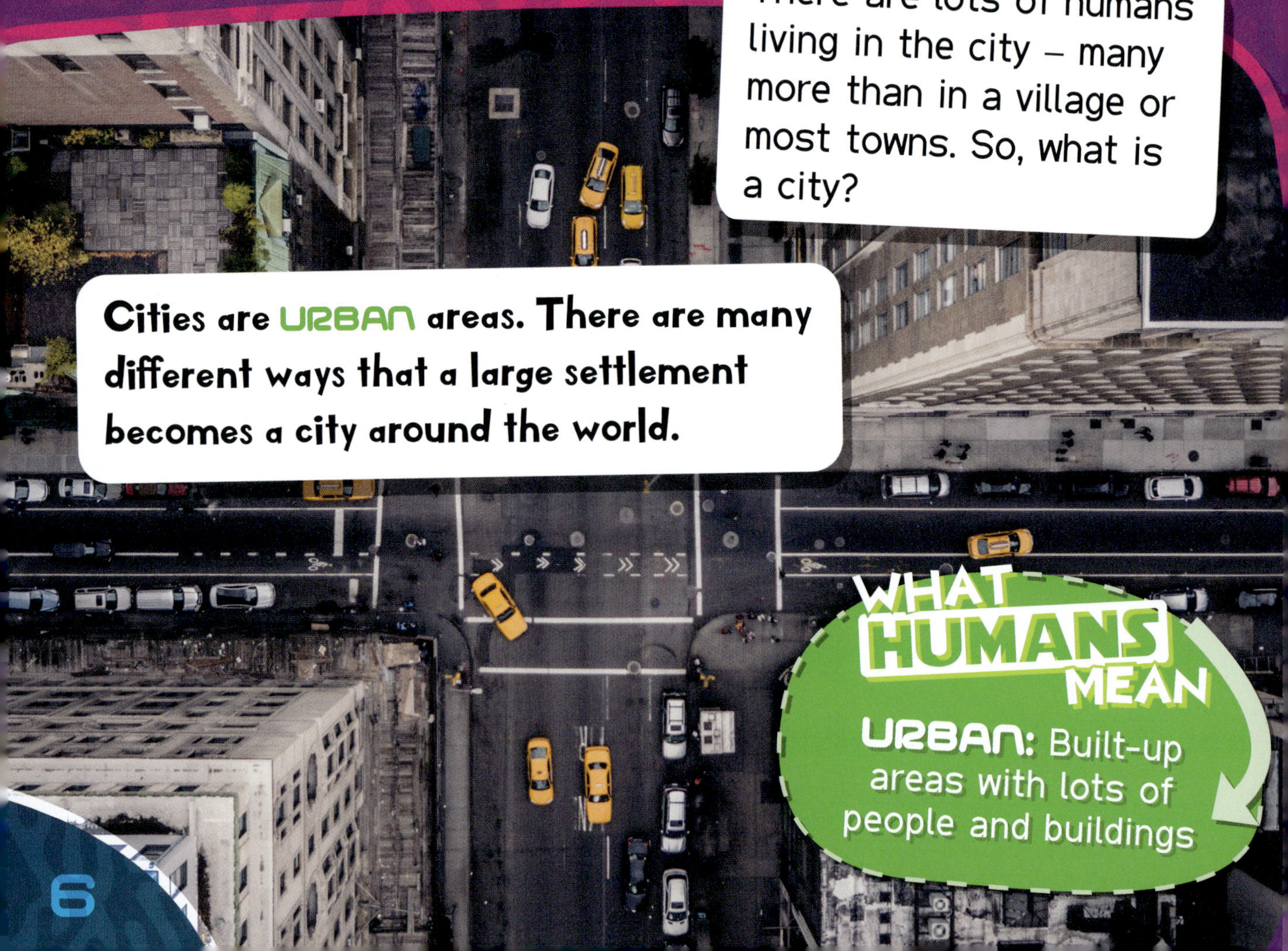

**Cities are URBAN areas. There are many different ways that a large settlement becomes a city around the world.**

## WHAT HUMANS MEAN

**URBAN:** Built-up areas with lots of people and buildings

In some places, a **cathedral** is one way a settlement becomes a city. Other parts of the world have different rules for what makes a place a city.

LINCOLN CATHEDRAL IN ENGLAND

# WHERE ARE THEY GOING?

If there is one thing you can say about a city, it is that there are lots of humans. They all look so busy. Many of these humans will live and work in the city. Others might travel here for fun or for work.

With such big **POPULATIONS**, cities need ways for these humans to get where they need to go. Cities have many roads and different **TRANSPORTATION SYSTEMS**.

## WHAT HUMANS MEAN

**POPULATIONS:** How many people live in certain places

**TRANSPORTATION SYSTEMS:** Ways to move people around, such as trains, subways, and buses

# WHAT IS IN A CITY?

Cities have lots of different buildings in them. I wondered what happens in them. So, I took a look in some. There are **RESIDENTIAL** buildings, **COMMERCIAL** buildings, and **GOVERNMENTAL** buildings.

CITY HALL

PLACES OF WORSHIP

Humans who belong to a **religion** use these places to **pray** and **worship**.

## WHAT HUMANS MEAN

**RESIDENTIAL:** Made for people to live in

**COMMERCIAL:** To do with making money

**GOVERNMENTAL:** To do with the government that runs a town, city, or country

**HOMES**

**STORES**

The buildings in cities are often very close together.

# HAVING FUN IN THE CITY

Since so many humans live here, cities need lots of places for humans to enjoy themselves. Humans have found many ways that they can have fun.

Humans often travel to visit cities for events, shows, and to enjoy the **CULTURE** of the city. Some humans fly across the world just to visit a city!

**WHAT HUMANS MEAN**

**CULTURE:** The traditions, ideas, and ways of life of a certain group of people

# SHOPPING IN THE CITY

Cities have all kinds of stores. Some stores sell things that every human needs, such as food and medicine. Other stores sell special things that humans can treat themselves with.

In cities, there are whole streets that are filled with stores. Some stores can be absolutely huge! Some humans spend whole days looking around these stores.

# CITY HALL

The city hall is a very important place in a city. It is where people living in the city come together and have meetings. They get to talk about how the city is being run.

Meetings at city hall can be about all kinds of things. Usually, they are about how humans can make their cities better. Most cities have a mayor. The mayor is a leader who works at city hall.

# SCHOOLS IN THE CITY

There are lots of humans in a city, which means there are many children. Many cities have a lot of schools for the children to go to.

Cities have schools for children of all ages. Many cities also have schools for adults who want to keep learning. These are called colleges and universities.

# BUSINESSES IN THE CITY

Settlements usually start because humans build around a business. Cities might start based on one business. As they get bigger and bigger, cities have more and more businesses in them.

Businesses help bring money into a city. They also give jobs to the humans living there. Some businesses **employ** hundreds of humans. Other businesses might only have a few humans working there.

# TUNE in NEXT WEEK

Well, aren't cities fascinating? I have spent a lot of time looking at cities, and there is still so much more to explore! I still have millions more humans in the cities to meet!

Cities, towns, and villages are all connected. Roads and railways link all of these places together. A city could be a lovely place to live... if you are a human!

# GLOSSARY

**CATHEDRAL** a large place of worship for some Christians

**EMPLOY** to give someone a job

**PRAY** to talk to a god or gods of a chosen belief

**RELIGION** an organized set of beliefs usually centered around a god or gods

**WORSHIP** a religious act where a person expresses praise for a god or gods

# INDEX